Phyllis Berenson

P9-DZX-952

Threads of Experience

Deidre Scherer's artwork has been featured on the following publications:

Anthologies
edited by Sandra Haldeman Martz

❧

When I Am an Old Woman I Shall Wear Purple
If I Had My Life to Live Over I Would Pick More Daisies
Grow Old Along with Me—The Best Is Yet to Be

Poetry

❧

Another Language by Sue Saniel Elkind

Caregiving

❧

Learning to Sit in the Silence: A Journal of Caretaking by Elaine Marcus Starkman

Threads of Experience

Fabric-and-Thread Images by Deidre Scherer

Edited by Sandra Haldeman Martz

Papier-Mache Press
Watsonville, California

Copyright © 1996 by Papier-Mache Press. Printed in Hong Kong. All rights reserved including the right to reproduce this book or portions thereof in any form. For information contact Papier-Mache Press, 135 Aviation Way, #14, Watsonville, CA 95076.

First Edition

00 99 98 97 96 5 4 3 2 1

ISBN: 0-918949-92-0 Hardcover

Cover art, "Treasure, © 1993 by Deidre Scherer

Interior fabric-and-thread images © by Deidre Scherer

Book design by Joyce Marie Kuchar

Composition by Leslie Austin and Joyce Marie Kuchar

Artist's photograph by Jeff Baird

Editor's photograph by Thomas Burke

Fabric-and-thread images photographed by Jeff Baird

Library of Congress Cataloging-in-Publication Data

Threads of experience / images by Deidre Scherer :
edited by Sandra Haldeman Martz. — 1st. ed.
p. cm.
ISBN 0-918949-92-0 (alk. paper)
1. Aged, Writings of the, American. 2. Old age—United States—Poetry.
3. Aged—United States—Poetry. 4. Aged—Portraits.
I. Scherer, Deidre, 1944– . II. Martz, Sandra.
PS591.A35T48 1996
811.008'0354—dc20   95-51733
CIP

To Sarenna, Corina, Gianna, and Ben,
and to Steve,
for believing in me

Foreword

There is something about cloth that is as basic as the air we breathe. It's connected with the necessities for survival: food, clothing certainly, and shelter. We instinctively understand it, because it surrounds us from birth until death. It appears fragile, but it is strong enough to power ships around the world. It is the stuff of celebrations and ceremonies, but it also binds our wounds and soaks up our body's fluids. It can be as stiff as a board or as supple as a caress. Like skin, it is an honest material, and that's why Deidre Scherer has chosen it to make her art. Why use paint, the medium in which she was trained, when cloth, a more sympathetic substance, can cut through our defenses and bind her images of aging to our hearts?

Just as life is built from layers of experience, Scherer builds her forms, cutting the cloth, layering it, assembling first with pins, and then securing the pieces with the sewing machine. For her, pieces of calico are the building blocks of her portraits, using either the bright printed front of the fabric or the lighter, shadowed back. Character, the spirit within each of her portraits, is developed as she layers and adjusts these pieces. The lines of machine stitching form the structure, holding the bits and pieces together, but she also uses these tiny stitches to add personal touches, a random strand of hair; the traces of accumulated smiles or frowns; the highlights in her subjects' eyes.

We are drawn into the work through the eyes, and then note the years, the attitude, the humanity of these people and their surroundings. Each face is so expressive: questioning, confronting, mocking, conspiring, laughing, surviving. Some seem so in the present moment; others lost in thought or the past. We wish to know these people, but the portraits can only tell us what we see, and so we substitute our own stories, project our thoughts, fears, and hopes about aging, living fully, dying gracefully.

Scherer is living a full life. Her children have children now. She's confronted a life-threatening illness and survived. Her work began in 1980 with a set of tarot cards. She searched for a model for the queens, someone with wisdom and experience, and found her in a nearby retirement home. And she found so much more there: a richness of life and death. She never returned to the tarot, but moved on to do images of aging.

In the process of knowing those who have sat for her, she has confronted her own thoughts and fears about aging and death, as well as our society's attitudes about aging. She has become involved in the hospice movement, which deals with and honors the transition from life to death. Her work has taken her to international locations, to museums and health care seminars, to hospitals and retirement facilities, and then back home to her family and attic studio.

Here she returns to the timeless images she cuts from cloth, stitching layers of emotion and layers of meaning into each work. Along with her subjects, we will also eventually fade and die, but the cloth will keep breathing their (and our) stories. For as one of the poets in this book notes: "Patches, like hand-me-downs, wear on."

— *Barbara Lee Smith*

Threads of Experience

Transcending

Essence

Sixty-eight years! I have survived
wars, depression, hunger,
unemployment,
loss of father, mother, child.
At last I am ready to live.

Now I see more clearly
the river of life flows onward.
People come and go,
friends, children, family,
like actors in a play.

What will tomorrow bring
or yet today what may I see?
There will be storms, drought,
heat waves, cool spring breezes.
Each will pass away.

The secret is revealed!
In each person, season, trial, and event
there is a lesson to be learned,
a quality to be savored.
Rejoice but do not cling too fast.

Seek the essence,
find the joy,
explore the exquisite pain,
taste depression and delight,
as each will pass your way.

─ Louise Ramsdell

Night Tide

Facing the Angels

I always wanted a room of them,
men with beards, wise faces,
women with thin smiles who listen
as part of a love affair gone brown.
The eyes have never been damaged
but stare down and through terror,
there is Einstein and Shaw,
and Jung and Georgia O'Keeffe,
and Whitman and Rabindranath Tagore.
Let them sit on my porch in Indiana
beside the pear tree that barely
makes it through winter, and talk
not about meaning but about growing old.
Let them tell me what awaits touching
for my body when it becomes a stick,
why longing hasn't killed them.
When I put up their photographs
I will pray for someone to lie down
beside me, as must be their good fortune,
and to whisper in everyone's lined ears:

Come, feed your soul the right food
and your brain will give you the right face.

— Rosaly DeMaios Roffman

Life Lines

As time etches lines
across my face,

may they read strength,
not weakness,

also patience,
especially with myself

as my feet slow in pace,
my hands grow clumsy.

May my image
still reflect pride

in the mirrors
along life's corridors.

When inertia sets in
may my spirit continue

to dance on sunlit lawns,
in moonlit memories.

~ Rose Mary Sullivan

Treasure

Saintly Line

Sonnet for Summer's Passing

I wander in a grand and rugged chasm,
my echoes roaring in a clanging din.
The years first dance themselves in whirl and spasm,
then spent, they lounge about the jagged bin.
Wine-colored summers spark a golden splinter;
disenchanted summers chilled by chance;
fleeting summers painted into winter;
laughing summers wild with spring's romance.
Many are my seasons now departed,
pressed into roles of daughter, mother, wife.
And for each self once lost or brokenhearted
up mounts a surging spring of light and life.

Don't ask for poems of summers long outworn,
for I would sing of seasons yet unborn.

— *Barbara Nector Davis*

Long Passage

If you conceive yourself
as a vessel, the first half you fill
with learning, lore, kids, the tensions
to keep the liquid at the brim
or over the top without spilling

The second half sees an emptying—
you handle death and its diminishments
voices fade in your ear
photographs retain faces otherwise lost
Because there is too much to remember
you can only forget

Where once I ran through days
my pace is now more composed
My appetite once insatiable
I now select with care
Once my eyes could not take in enough
now if I stare into darkness
I find it less frightening, knowing
all darkness is not ahead

When I do not sleep at night
I can nap in the day
Birds still twitter at first light

— *Ruth F. Eisenberg*

Thresholds

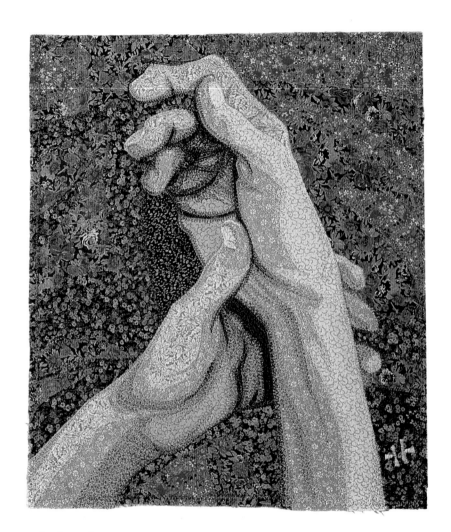

Floral Hands

For Touching

The old woman sat quietly, gently rocking herself as she looked down on her hands. "They still look young," she thought, "such long, slender fingers."

"You have piano hands," her mother used to say. Her fingers could span one octave, and she had liked the graceful movements of hands across ivory.

"Give me your hand," a man had said many years ago and had slipped a gold band on her finger. It once held much promise.

"Hold my hand!" a small child had begged and had reached up to take two of her fingers. She missed the touch of small hands.

"I love your hands," an artist had once said. "I'd like to draw them." But then he never did. Surely her hands weren't worthy of an artist's study.

"Your hands are made for touching and caressing," someone else had said. He had had a way with words, and she had believed him.

Now her hands lay across her lap, hands which had worked and loved and were growing tired.

"But they still look young," she thought and put her hand against her cheek.

— Claudia Logerquist

Third Light

Reading Your History

Last night's snow interprets the hills
their sloping definitions; and today
the creases you've gathered
over the years as tiny grooves

define your life as now the far-branching
limbs outside our window sketch the oak,
the way it has chosen to part the air
on the north side of the house.

Each furrow in your brow catching
the faintest shadow traces a memory
held long enough to leave its mark,
as a stream over time wears

a seam in the earth. Your face is a maze
I explore, a map that explains your past,
as veins of lightning on a stormy night
expose a whole landscape, or nerves

forking the end of a muscle determine
a certain movement for a lifetime.
This morning I am reading your history—
pain, the worry of hard work, and the curves

of laughter. Were you younger,
I would have had less time to love you,
would have less braille to decipher
as I gather your stories beneath my fingertips.

— Pam Noble

Taking Inventory

Tonight,
who I was turns
into who I am,
and I notice my hands,
each one weathered,
gnarled as a tree branch
but still reaching out to teach me
the braille of touching.

But eyes,
what's to become of you?
Theater of all I see
turned inward now,
away from the world,
bringing this strange flow
of spidery webs
and phantom lights,
preparation, perhaps,
for everything passing
that can't be explained.

And joints
I've taken too much for granted,
you who make possible
each of my gestures,
obedient servants
for so many years of bending,
it's high time for me to share
your unspoken language of pain.

~ *Marilyn M. Williams*

Firelight

Fragments

Strings of Heat

He cannot see the flakes but, from inside his dark
house, hears the hush of their thick fall and pulls
his sweater closer. When he releases the catch
on his watch crystal and touches the hands

underneath, he sees it is too early for bed, so he sits
in a kitchen chair, listening for a long time to the stillness
until he is so cold he retreats to the hall closet, feels
for the coarse wool of his coat, chases a scarf as it falls

into the front left corner, and there he discovers
the dusty case of his abandoned cello. When he snaps
open the cool metal latches, he is wrapped in the warm
smell of rosin and wood. He draws out the bow, lifts

the instrument by its slender neck and plucks and twists
to bring it into tune. Finally he hugs its curves
between his legs and massages its strings for the fire
of its familiar voice—how had he forgotten.

~ Linda Fuller-Smith

bridge hand

fingers sighing afternoons
the old woman hides
in a game   one club

her hand whispers
queens and aces   two diamonds

translucent skin blankets
blue veins   oriental willow
decorates a child's plate   two no trump

brittle nails done up like dolls
dance toward game   three hearts

rings dangle from skinny fingers
skewed at graceless angles
by swollen knuckles   five diamonds

her fingers flutter
anticipating tricks   double

she drums the table
finesses favors from the gods   makes a small slam

the pencil marks the score
the line is drawn   vulnerable

her hands still   birds
wanting to cross over into flight
wait again for the deal   play the game

— Lianne Elizabeth Mercer

Minnie Amalia

The Last Wild Strawberry

Twosome

The Not Said

The calico cat, between
us, stretches
on the couch, rolls
on her back, seizes
first you, then me,
two aging women,
with her animal eyes.
By turns we stroke
the whiteness
between her black
limbs. Her front paws,
orange, flare and push
slowly into the air,
as if it were pushing
back. Not talking yet
we watch
each other's hands
caress her trunk, her tail
wave up and curl.
"I like her body," you say
at last. Your fingers skim
her dugs. "When one lives
alone," you say, not
looking at me, "one comes
to want something
like this."

— *Kay Barnes*

Sisters, Too

Two Sisters at Dinner

White linen cloth
silver candlesticks, pink roses
in a crystal bowl. Ada comes
out of the kitchen, sets a steaming
casserole on the table. She
remembers to take off her apron.
Lucy smoothes her faded black dress
tucks back a wisp of hair
draws tight the velvet drapes.
They sit down, and the candles
begin to flicker as their soft voices
breathe out memories of travel
in foreign lands; of youth
and family, suitors loved,
laughed with, even cried over.

Their words run into each other
sentences hang unfinished in the air
each story known by heart:
remembered joy, remembered sorrow.
But none of it matters now.
What matters is the pleasure
in the telling and the miracle
of days undimmed by mounting years.
Two sisters at dinner.
With fragile hands they lift
their glasses pale with wine,
replace the gutted candles,
retell the stories.

— Eleanor Byers

The Walker

I am used to this, Richard's
impatience all the way to my room
when he visits. Yet God knows

I'm no tortoise. I'll never get used
to the walker. None of the young
look at the truth: my knees, not

my mind, make me slow. How my head
swims with concerns: hot tea and muffins,
sure. But also pollution, ice storms,

the Middle East. Who can I trust
with Grandmother's coin silver spoons.
Keeping my mail to myself, finding

a clerk: you'd think eighty was dead.
This morning, another one went.
If they don't go before dawn then

it's five in the evening with day
on the edge of memory. Dusk always
has brought me up short: time escaping,

is this all I will know? And night
hovers behind like a dream of murder.
There is my room, Richard hurrying ahead.
He forgets each day he is older.

~ Elizabeth Follin-Jones

Afternoon Sun

Questions

illiterati

I learn them often only
thus; weathered, withered
parchment skin; dead
sea scrolls; steroid
tried and negligibly thin…

upon these pages traced in purple
varicosities: what past, what
peril faced; what bold
audacities: moments held
transfixed by breeze insinuating
spring; what firm determination in the
face of winter wind; what laughter,
sorrow; loves and loss…

I cannot read
this whispered litany of
yesterdays in the raucous
crossing of a
last tomorrow…

countless tales of revelry and
rages; silently untold on
turning pages; I learn
the texture of the skin; the anonymity
of ages…

I learn to not
conjecture of their youth; never
trespass to the private heresy
of truth; to dare no
deeper, not traverse
the scripture's binding to
the secrets

for if each death
disclosed, in verse or
prose, the life it took: what hand
could daily bear to
turn the pages of this book?

— David Katz, MD

Patchwork

She stitched little squares because she hated
throwing anything away: housedresses
and boxer shorts, scraps too gay to be dustcloths,
rescued from the ragman and reborn.

She squints at the Rose of Sharon appliquéd
from her wedding dress. Her heart swells
as she clutches the sateen bouquets. Sixty years
of marriage. She scales Jacob's Ladder,
her husband's Sunday-go-to-meeting ties,
and longs to climb higher, higher, sleep
with him again. She weeps over Job's Tears—
the Slave Chain her grandmother wore
on her deathbed—links threadbare with sacrifice.
The crib-sized comforter—Tumbling Blocks
she cradles—was pieced from petticoats for her firstborn—
stillborn. In a gooseneck rocker, she unfolds
heirlooms, linens that summered in her hope chest,
releasing scents of cedar, spirits of kinfolk.

What becomes of faith when you outlive those you love?
Patches, like hand-me-downs, wear on. Draping
her lap, a quilted geography, terrain of textures;
valleys at her fingertips and Glory beyond.
The Evening Star, frayed, is leading her home.

~ Carole Boston Weatherford

Flower Bed

Still Friends

How It Ends

Slender and convoluted as the roots
of a Chinese snow pea planted in clay,
tunneling white tendrils down to absorb
nourishment, sending two oval leaves
up to begin a cycle of new growth.
You and I are friends.

Summer sunlight warms young green leaves.
The plant flourishes, tender pea pods
sugar sweet hang from every stem.
You and I are lovers.

Now I watch sleet cover the ground.
Geese fly south deserting icy ponds
and the children who ran eagerly to feed
them leftover crumbs. The snow pea plant
freezes into a mass of twisted brown.
You and I are old.

— *Fran Portley*

Evensong for Amanda

Fragile as the shadow
pine-tipped long across the grass,
Amanda waits, eyes measuring the autumn sun
resting low on Raven Cliffs.
In the field beyond the house,
the hay rake stands abandoned,
its rust-brown wheels woven through
with goldenrod, tied to weedy earth.
Young pines are thrusting up
where corn once grew in clean-hoed rows
and beans wrapped waving arms
around tassels, brushing past tawny silks.

Leaning on her knobby stick, Amanda clucks shame
on the apple tree falsely pink in April,
promising fruit that turned to gnarled lumps
worm-pocked and ribbed on twisted limbs.
She remembers plump red globes and jelly
clear as amber glass shining on cupboard shelves.

Behind the apple tree, the barn slumps tires
from the green embrace of kudzu vines,
and two old banty hens scratch for beetles,
raising spurts of soft red dust.
Sun down, Amanda turns, climbs the ragged steps
and sits on the porch to rock a while.
Creaking floorboards and a catbird, crickets
and old hens sing for her, a solitary song.

— Bettie M. Sellers

Reflecting

no place like

keep moving
hips like rusty gates today
legs like shaky stilts and canes no help
at 81 you have to keep on moving   can't let
your daughter see you wincing trembling
that home she talks about well that's
no place for me
no room for Mother's hutch
my wedding suite Bill's paintings
heart pounds so loud it hurts   oh
          talk to her now
tell her something   Mrs. Jacobs's new azalea
cats dug up the tulip bulbs   no
I think I told her that already
where did I put the bills   don't let
her see you searching   *did* I
already tell her?
          hide the broken plate
and keep on moving can't sit down
it's a lot of trouble getting up these days
sometimes almost

too much trouble but can't sit here forever

stop moving and she'll move me out

that home's no place
for me no place at all   those old people
sitting staring giving up
keep moving keep those joints working
bones grinding biting on each other
no I don't need any
help dear
          now what's she looking at the nosy girl
those prying ways that's her father's family

doctor's appointment   no that's tomorrow
not today   I'm sure it's tomorrow

oh

well I was just so busy
anybody could forget a thing like that anybody
could forget   I'll phone and   no   let me
I'll do it   heart hurts   this is my house
my house

— *Sue Nevill*

Map of the Year One Hundred

Old Friends

Talking to Angels

In the clay red of dusk,
as light sifts down the hills
behind the barn,
he sits with his coffee cup
and watches sparrows
rest on the wire.
The same birds
built nests in the windmill
fifty years ago.
He frames his life
by the kitchen window,
looks south past the silo's sign,
"Smith and Sons" repainted
even after the boys left home
and the fields became someone else's.
A mare still grazes near the fence,
head down, content in sweet grass.
The sunset soaks into the iris of his eye
as he leans toward eighty.
"Well, good night then. See you tomorrow,"
he says out loud, and no one answers or
the answer is clear and comforting
and the voice of someone dear.

— Kathleen Patrick

Morning Song

I feel as if, sometimes, I am the meadowlark.
Awaking with the sun, my voice fills the day
and the farmer husband goes to the backbreaking chore of
planting.
I plant in our children the property of hard work
The value of honesty. I plant in them the seed of hope
not despair, I sing to them like the meadowlark.
And the farmer husband goes to the gentle art of
thinning.
Thin the good from the bad, the weak from the strong.
To teach my children sacrifices, to give up what cannot
be. So all the remaining plants and ideals
can stand straight and tall in the prairie sun.
They sing to me the sad song of meadowlarks.
And the farmer husband goes to the final task of
reaping.

The children take up their wings and leave.
One takes a wife, one heads for college
one works in town.
But all return to help at harvest, all teach their
children to sow good crops.
At night we lay with our grey heads together
and we listen for the sweet song of the meadowlarks.

⌐ *Nancy Bennett*

Conjunction

Maria in Memory

Harvesting Mellow

I've harvested days
from low-lying branches,
years from each above,
and learned that green
was seldom so sweet
as fruit from seasoned wood.

I've plucked wild berries
heavy on vines,
eaten past hunger or need,
and found that gluttony
feeds on self
and leaves a gluttonous want.

When I was young
and greedy to grasp
all the bounty ahead,
I trampled time
seeding dreams:
would tomorrow never come?

But harvesting now
from dwindling stores,
I taste each day
with a connoisseur's tongue
and slowly savor
rich, rare time
sweetened by many suns.

~ Helen Friedland

Talking to Herself

Of course I'm not just saving seed,
kneeling here, snapping off dried-up heads
of marigolds. I'm saying this old wizened plant
has plenty in her yet. Sure, she has earned
her rest, but look, each head is like
a quiverful, and every arrow knows
the way to root and bloom. She'll pack
a wallop. Just you wait and see.

Of course I'm not just planting bulbs,
kneeling here, digging my holes and stuffing
these beggars in and heaping up dirt.
I'm saying, Yes, he died. He's buried,
but we're planted so deep down together,
winter's never going to get us.
Give us time. We'll be a sight
for sore eyes. Just you wait and see.

— Helen Weaver Horn

In the Garden

Mid-Sentence

Only in Dreams

She sits, rigid, eyes dart
    laser-bright, wary as a wren—
a thin smile trickles across her face
    to appease the public eye
but it is her feet that tell us
    there is a churning inside,
the ankle twisting the foot
    in endless circles, fenced-in soul
that yearns to break the boundaries—
    she hugs herself, reins in those
passions that beat against her breast
    erupt inside with a storm
that astonishes her when she
    asks, "What have I done with these
eighty years?" and her spirit
    springs free to dream, leap, and twirl,
her fantasies rise like old ghosts,
    they dance again on her heart
kneading it like bread dough until
    a thin veil slides over her eyes
and her feet are quiet at last.

— Charlotte A. Coté

On Aging

(After Kahlil Gibran)

Then an elder of the city said, Speak to us of Aging.

And he answered:

To age is to witness the unfolding of the seed of life's eternal wisdom. Just as the aged cannot regain the youth of the body, so also does the newborn babe know nothing of the wisdom that life awaits to reveal. For what remembrance has the tender bud of the fruit of the harvest? And only by going forth to the harvest can the spirit be one again with the seed that gave it life.

The aged are the stewards of life's secrets. They are the keepers of the images of the waking dream as it is dreamed in the mind of God.

While youth treads an unfamiliar path that seems endless, the aged see the endless circle of life's path returning unto itself.

Time does not tarry for those who are reluctant to yield to age, or quicken its tempo for those who have wearied of life. Neither does time change its course for those who would leave the path of life to turn their desire toward yesterday.

The aged stand at the crossroads of eternity and the decay of that which is bound by the chains of time. To choose the eternal is to fulfill the vision that was conceived before the foundation of the earth, and cast aside the withering seed that the spirit may soar to the boundless realm where the body cannot go.

~ *Catherine Ismail*

Myth Maker

About the Artworks

"Transcending," April 1995, 11″ x 10″
© 1995 by Deidre Scherer

"Night Tide," July 1993, 8″ x 7″
© 1993 by Deidre Scherer

"Treasure," January 1993, 11″ x 10″
© 1993 by Deidre Scherer

"Saintly Line," February 1995, 9″ x 8″
© 1995 by Deidre Scherer

"Thresholds," July 1993, 11″ x 9″
© 1993 by Deidre Scherer

"Floral Hands," February 1993, 11″ x 10″
© 1993 by Deidre Scherer

"Third Light," September 1990, 7$\frac{1}{2}$″ x 7″
© 1990 by Deidre Scherer

"Firelight," October 1993, 11″ x 10″
© 1993 by Deidre Scherer

"Fragments," June 1987, 26″ x 22″
© 1987 by Deidre Scherer

"Minnie Amalia," November 1982, 21$\frac{1}{4}$″ x 17$\frac{1}{4}$″
© 1982 by Deidre Scherer

"The Last Wild Strawberry," June 1989, 32″ x 53″
© 1989 by Deidre Scherer

"Sisters, Too," July 1992, 23″ x 18″
© 1992 by Deidre Scherer

"Twosome," January 1991, 29$\frac{1}{2}$″ x 22″
© 1991 by Deidre Scherer

"Afternoon Sun," September 1988, 26″ x 22″
© 1988 by Deidre Scherer

"Questions," June 1987, 35″ x 34″
© 1987 by Deidre Scherer

"Flower Bed," August 1983, 41$\frac{1}{2}$″ x 32$\frac{1}{2}$″
© 1983 by Deidre Scherer

"Still Friends," June 1993, 11″ x 10″
© 1993 by Deidre Scherer

"Reflecting," August 1994, 11″ x 10″
© 1994 by Deidre Scherer

"Map of the Year One Hundred," March 1987,
23$\frac{1}{2}$″ x 23″ © 1987 by Deidre Scherer

"Old Friends," February 1992, 22″ x 19″
© 1992 by Deidre Scherer

"Conjunction," January 1995, 12″ x 12″
© 1995 by Deidre Scherer

"Maria in Memory," June 1983, 23$\frac{1}{2}$″ x 19″
© 1983 by Deidre Scherer

"In the Garden," February 1993, 24″ x 17″
© 1993 by Deidre Scherer

"Mid-Sentence," February 1990, 32″ x 21″
© 1990 by Deidre Scherer

"Myth Maker," July 1993, 11″ x 9″
© 1993 by Deidre Scherer

About the Artist

DEIDRE SCHERER grew up in the woods of New York state in a family of artists. She received her BFA from the Rhode Island School of Design in 1967. A cloth book she made for her three daughters inspired her to substitute cloth for paint, and she has worked with fabric and thread since then. Her images of aging have appeared in more than ninety individual and group shows throughout the United States and internationally, and her work has graced the covers of five Papier-Mache Press books. She is sincerely grateful to all of the women and men who have inspired the images in this book—without whose wisdom and strength her work would not be possible.

About the Editor

SANDRA HALDEMAN MARTZ, founding editor of Papier-Mache Press, has compiled numerous successful collections exploring women's issues and the art of growing older. Her pioneering work in exploring important social issues through literature has helped to redefine the role of poetry and fiction in the lives of everyday people.

About the Contributors

KAY BARNES, a graduate of the Vermont College MFA program in writing and the French School of Middlebury College, translates contemporary French poetry, writes freelance articles, and leads poetry workshops in Dallas, Texas.

NANCY BENNETT, a history enthusiast, is researching a book on Canadian pioneer women of color (Green Dragon Press). She grew up in the small farming communities of Saskatchewan, where her poem has its roots, and now lives with her husband and two daughters in Victoria, British Columbia.

ELEANOR BYERS lives in Coeur D'Alene, Idaho, where she is active in the local chapter of the Idaho Writer's League. She is a graduate of Washington State University.

CHARLOTTE A. COTÉ, poet and author of *Olympia Brown: The Battle for Equality* (Mother Courage Press), is researching a new biography of the mother of the Equal Rights Amendment, Alice Paul. She received her MA from the University of Wisconsin-Milwaukee.

BARBARA NECTOR DAVIS is an editor, poet, playwright, and novelist. Her publishing credits include a poetry and photo collaboration with her photographer husband, Robert Martin Davis.

RUTH F. EISENBERG, as a teacher, urged a respect for formal structural demands and the importance of fact but with poetry, she could conjure a line and then see what surprises it would reveal; that's having the best of both worlds. Ms. Eisenberg died in 1996 at the age of sixty-nine.

ELIZABETH FOLLIN-JONES, a graduate of the University of Michigan in mathematics, didn't begin writing until after she was fifty. She is also a fiction writer and sculpts in papier-mache.

HELEN FRIEDLAND, a graduate of New York University and Columbia University, is a poet, writer, and editor, and has been a guest lecturer at numerous university poetry workshops, literature classes, and extension programs.

LINDA FULLER-SMITH, formerly a professional ballet dancer, teacher, and costumer, is a published poet. An Ohio native, she has also lived in Italy and California where she studied creative writing at Long Beach City College.

HELEN WEAVER HORN, a writer, teacher, and community counselor, lives with her husband on a small cattle farm in Appalachian Ohio and has one daughter. She has been active in Quaker meetings and the peace movement all her life. She has collected oral histories of elderly women from local mining towns.

CATHERINE ISMAIL lives with her husband, Mohammed, and their children, Jason, Sarah, and Michael, in the high desert of rural southern Arizona. Writing and music are spices in her life of running a business and raising a family.

DAVID KATZ, MD, is assistant clinical professor of medicine at Yale University. His poem is a product of his experience with aging, and its inevitable consequences, in the clinical setting.

CLAUDIA LOGERQUIST is a new creative writer, but spends most of her time teaching English to children from other countries. She was born and raised in Germany, and writes in English as her second language. Her home is in Boulder, Colorado.

LIANNE ELIZABETH MERCER does collages to spark her creative process and to help enhance the images and connections in her fiction and poetry. Her chapbook, *No Limits But Light*, was published by Chili Verde Press in 1994.

SUE NEVILL's poetry appears regularly in Canadian literary periodicals. Her first book, *I Was Expecting Someone Taller*, was published in 1991. She lives in Vancouver, British Columbia.

PAM NOBLE is a poet, psychotherapist, and spiritual director, and is cofounder of Interweave, an organization that promotes interaction between poetry and the arts. She lives on a ridge in the Blue Ridge Mountains of North Carolina.

KATHLEEN PATRICK, whose work has received several awards, wrote this poem for her grandfather, the father of ten children, who used to recite poetry all the time.

FRAN PORTLEY majored in English Honors at Duke University and now teaches poetry to children in the New Jersey Joining Old and Young (JOY) program.

LOUISE RAMSDELL, a seventy-one-year-old retired social worker, devotes her energies to exploring the creative arts, to wit: poetry, creative writing, watercolor painting, and playing the cello in preparation for her next incarnation.

ROSALY DEMAIOS ROFFMAN is developing a myth and folklore center at the Indiana University of Pennsylvania, where she teaches. She is coeditor of *Life on the Line: Healing and Words*, and the second edition of her poetry book, *Going to Bed Whole*, was released in 1994.

BETTIE M. SELLERS, poet and professor of English at Young Harris College, Georgia, is the producer of an award-winning documentary film on the life and works of Byron Herbert Reece.

ROSE MARY SULLIVAN, a repatriated native of Connecticut after living many years in the Southwest and California, is known among her friends as the "Grandma Moses of poetry."

CAROLE BOSTON WEATHERFORD is a poet, children's book author, and mother. A Maryland native and North Carolina resident, she treasures the quilt her grandmother made. Her books include *The Tan Chanteuse* and *Juneteenth Jamboree*.

MARILYN M. WILLIAMS was born in Washington, DC, but as an army brat lived in many states. She has three children and taught nursery school for twenty-one years. A graduate of Washington University in St. Louis, her writing was inspired by Donald Finkel and his wife, Constance Urdang.

Acknowledgments

Grateful acknowledgment is made to the following publications which first published some of the material in this book: *Amber* © 1994 for "Morning Song" by Nancy Bennett; *Journal of the American Medical Association*, 271:1890m, 1994, for "illiterati" by David Katz, MD; *The New Quarterly*, vol. IX, no. 4, Winter 1989 and *I Was Expecting Someone Taller* (Beach Holme Publishing) © 1991 for "no place like" by Sue Nevill; *Morning of the Red-Tailed Hawk* (Green River Press) © 1981 for "Evensong for Amanda" by Bettie Sellers; and *The Tan Chanteuse* (North Carolina Writers' Network) for "Patchwork" by Carole Boston Weatherford.

Grateful acknowledgment is made to the following photographers whose work inspired some of Deidre Scherer's images in this collection: Hansi Durlack from *The Short Season of Sharon Springs* (© 1980 by Cornell University Press) for "Minnie Amalia"; Diana Davies from *Photojourney* (Bag Lady Press, © 1989 by Diana J.M. Davies) for "The Last Wild Strawberry"; Jon Gilbert Fox from *Vermonters* (The Countryman Press, photos © 1985 by Jon Gilbert Fox) for Twosome"; Pamela Valois from *Gifts of Age* (© 1985 Chronicle Books) for "Afternoon Sun"; Ann Zane Shanks from *Old Is What You Get* (The Viking Press, © 1976 by Ann Zane Shanks) for "Questions"; John Willis for "Reflecting"; Peter Miller from *Vermont People* (Vermont People Project, © 1990 by Peter Miller) for "Old Friends"; Karen L. Thalin for "Conjunction"; Susan Sichel from *The Other Side* (© 1979 by Doubleday & Co.) for "Maria in Memory"; and Sonia Cullinen for "In the Garden."

Grateful acknowledgment is made to the following people whose collections include some of Deidre Scherer's images in this book. From the collection of: Roger W. Himler for "Transcending" and "Floral Hands"; Marilyn and Irwin Scher for "Treasure"; Judith Green for "Saintly Line" and "Conjunction"; Tom Sawyer and Jeffrey Anne Ligenza for "Third Light"; Michael Anderko for "Firelight"; Theodora L. and Stanley H. Feldberg for "Fragments" and "Flower Bed"; David and Pamela Mayer for "Minnie Amalia"; The A.D.S. Group for "Sisters, Too" and "Old Friends"; Margery E. Feldberg for "Questions"; Nancy and Raymond Konkol for "Still Friends"; Deborah E. Kruger for "Reflecting"; James J. McGovern for "Map of the Year 100"; Sonia and George Cullinen for "Maria in Memory"; Annabel D. Edwards for "In the Garden"; Jonathan and Mary Ranshohoff for "Myth Maker"; and to the private owners of "Night Tide," "Thresholds," "The Last Wild Strawberry," Twosome," "Afternoon Sun," and "Mid-Sentence."

Papier=Mache Press

At Papier-Mache Press, it is our goal to identify and successfully present important social issues through enduring works of beauty, grace, and strength and to encourage empathy and respect among diverse communities.

We appreciate you, our customer, and strive to earn your continued support. We are especially grateful to the independent booksellers and gift store owners whose presence ensures a continuing diversity of opinion, information, and literature. We encourage our readers to support these stores with your patronage.

We publish many fine books and gift items. Please ask your local book or gift store about the Papier-Mache items they carry. To receive a complete catalog, send a self-addressed stamped envelope to Papier-Mache Press, Customer Service Department, 135 Aviation Way, #14, Watsonville, CA 95076, or call our toll-free customer service number, 800-927-5913